The Rainbow's Quivering Tongue

– *Stride* –

Other Stride anthologies:

A Curious Architecture: a selection of contemporary prose poems
edited by David Miller and Rupert Loydell

How The Net Is Gripped: a selection of contemporary American Poetry
edited by David Miller and Rupert Loydell

The Stumbling Dance: 21 poets
edited by Rupert M. Loydell

Jewels & Binoculars: fifty poets celebrate Bob Dylan
edited by Phil Bowen

Completing The Picture: exiles, outsiders & independents
edited by William Oxley

Things We Said Today: poems about The Beatles
edited by Phil Bowen

Stonechat: ten Devon poets
edited by Christopher Southgate

Ladder To The Next Floor: Stride Magazine 1-33
edited by Rupert M. Loydell (University of Salzburg Press)

Other Stride books by authors in this anthology:

Paper Birds Alison Chisholm

Lost Stations Jennie Fontana

Intimate Relations Louise Hudson

Snowfruit Mary Maher

Cold Flushes Mary Maher

In The Mirror Of Your Eyes Jane Tresidder

Other books by the editor:

Bread And Milk

For The Owl Man

THE RAINBOW'S QUIVERING TONGUE

an anthology of women's poetry

edited by

Mary Plain

THE RAINBOW'S
QUIVERING TONGUE

First edition 1995

ISBN 1 873012 85 86 1

Cover design by Joe Pieczenko

Published by
Stride Publications
11 Sylvan Road, Exeter,
Devon EX4 6EW

Contents

Introduction *6*

Chris Banks *7*
Judi Benson *11*
Stephanie Bowgett *16*
Debjani Chatterjee *21*
Alison Chisholm *25*
Rose Flint *29*
Jennie Fontana *35*
Linda France *42*
Sarah Hopkins *48*
Libby Houston *54*
Louise Hudson *60*
Judith Kazantzis *66*
Mary Maher *74*
Val Pancucci *80*
Joan Poulson *87*
Wendy Richmond *92*
Susan Sheppard *97*
Penelope Shuttle *103*
Sandra Stevens *109*
Susan Taylor *114*
Jane Tresidder *119*
Irena Uderska *125*
Ruth Valentine *130*

Contributors *134*

Acknowledgements *138*

INTRODUCTION

It's always a surprise when people take poetry seriously, and it was even more of a surprise to be asked to edit this book so soon after meeting Rupert Loydell, who runs Stride Publications. Discussing women's poetry – or should I say, attacking Stride for it's lack of women writers, and criticising the last Stride women's anthology *Frankenstein's Daughter* – resulted in the ball being quickly returned to my part of the court. "You do better: I need the manuscript by Spring."

Here's what I came up with. A mixture of new and established writers, a mixture of attitudes, stances and styles. For a while I wanted to call this anthology *Learning To Be Tough*, but that seemed to give off an aggressive air I didn't want, because I love the mix of domestic, trivial, earth-shattering, emotional, reckless, and safe poetry that people in this anthology have written. I'm not one for any notion of 'sisterhood', but I do demand an equal hearing as women – very different women writing in different ways to different audiences. *Reckless Seasoning* was on the shortlist of titles too, with its spiciness, and ideas of freedom ('recklessness') and overtones of our words changing the taste of male-dominated literature. I liked *The Easiest Sum In The Whole World* too, but one and one *isn't* the easiest sum in the world, and I didn't want this collection to be dismissed as women's love poems, despite there being plenty of work about relationships in the book.

So I went for the quivering tongue. Gossip and talk are sometimes seen as weaknesses, but we should, perhaps, celebrate them as an open form of communication. We share our feelings, talk things through, exercise our tongues, laugh, bicker, sing and shout; there are sexual overtones, too: the pleasures of licking and kissing. And the rainbow? Well, religious or not, it's a symbol of hope in our troubled world. Hope that maybe if we share and talk enough we can get those who won't talk or listen to somehow see the reality of how we live, how people interrelate, our very society in fact.

I don't really believe poetry in itself changes anything – but it may lead to change. It has to go hand in hand with the giving of our very selves to those who need help most. The poetry, too, must be given freely – this work was sent to me, I pass it on to you, hoping you'll both learn and enjoy.

Mary Plain

Chris Banks

TOUGH

Today I am learning to be tough.

Yesterday, you told me to piss off.
And lots besides. Words
I don't remember as words, but as thrown knives
that thunked home in my heart.
So today I am learning to be tough.

I hitched a long ride out on the motorway
to this service station,
where I sit at a table for one, smoking
my very first cigarette.
My eyes are narrowed and my legs are spread.

Already I can outstare anybody who looks at me.
Sorry, excuse me,
I don't mind: three phrases I've dropped
from my vocabulary.
My new hobby is seeing how far I can spit.

This jumper I am wearing is too soft. I plan
to dress in Docs
with everything. Buckles and black leather.
I have learnt
to let the swing door swing and bugger off.

I snatch a daddy-long-legs from the air
and tear it dead.
I'll smoke a pack of twenty cigarettes one day
and not feel sick.
From my thickened skin, your words will ricochet.

SEARCHING / LOST

What are you frightened of? she said.
His brown eyes darted away like fish.
She wanted to catch them, hold them,
see herself there, clearly reflected.

She could still feel the place where
his lips had brushed over her naked foot.
Don't, she'd said, pulling away, aching.
She knew how flesh speaks only easy words.

The moon filled the skylight, curious,
smiling. He sank in his leather chair,
taking a long drink. *Tell me*, she said,
who you are, what you are thinking of.

He showed her the photographs; each was
an image of who he might be. For props
he had used women and cars, but turned
from them all, unsmiling, detached.

He was so distant, lost. She followed
him then, with her lips, with her tongue –
knowing that when they had finished
and morning began, they both would be gone.

DEFENDING THE CASTLE

(From Boccaccio's painting 'Des Cleres et Nobles Femmes')

From the heart of the painted battle, she
flames out: Boccaccio's surprise.

All castle horizontals point towards where she
is poised on horseback. There

the eye must follow. Against her orange dress
and hair, how milky-skinned she is.

Her fellow soldiers, men encased in clumsy armour,
fight their own oppressors. She

has no protection, but her face says, *yes,*
I'm going to do this thing.

She grips a keen sword in her uplifted hand.
Her left lies lightly

on the shoulder of the enemy, as if to say,
Excuse me. Yes, I do mean you.

A man's head's about to roll. Her canny horse
sees this and twinkles.

Sometimes it happens that a woman knows the blade
must slice away whatever stands

between herself and freedom. Above the castle,
blue sky darkens, punctured

by a sisterhood of golden stars. A new moon,
honed like a sickle, smiles.

THE WOMAN WHO LOVED TOO MUCH

She loved a man with eyes of ice
who made of her a sacrifice.

She loved a man with fists of stone.
He bruised her body to the bone.

She met a man with arms of steel.
He held her till she could not feel.

And when each one had flung her down
she met a man who kissed her wounds

And made a harbour of his heart
to shelter her from any hurt.

But all his words of truth and love
bewildered her – she had to leave.

She found a man with eyes of ice
who made of her a sacrifice.

Judi Benson

OFF THE RAILS

Tonight he is leaving me,
going to that crazy country of babble borders
funny money that buys nothing
where the weather changes every minute.
Soft snow falling in a desert heat.

I watch him pack his bag of thorny bits
white anger burning through love words
slicing the quiet. What else does he take?
Nothing practical, no compass, no clock.
There is no direction. Time is a crazy hand on a faceless dial.

He slips backwards, forwards, twenty years ago – yesterday.
There is no tomorrow.
Now is the standstill place he won't let me stand still in.
Come here, he says, hold me. Just so he can push me away
so he can say, you never hold me, why don't you just hold me?

Will I see him off? Stand on the shore waving his boat away
mouthing reminders: write me when you get there,
take care, take care. Futile words that don't belong
on this trip he takes
to the nowhere place of bad dreams no one else is in.

THE ASSIGNMENT

Mr. Green said, *explore the colour red*
50 shades laid out on white paper.
I licked my brush, thought of autumn leaves, cherries, apples,
mangoes, a certain shade of lipstick, nail gloss
sun sinking into the sea, blood on the water,
roses, tulips, rubies, robins
fire flickering a second before blue
the heart, a muscle, raw meat
colour of the inside places, warning lights
stop signs, fire engines, life coming, life going
quickly on high heels
colour of a scream cutting through the night.

CALL WAITING

My son on the other line, his echo of "I'm fine",
reading Dostoevsky in the desert between war games and grenades
absently tossed, eyes closed missing the target – Idiot!
he shouts to himself. All day in 150 degree weather
with the tankety clank noise, sun burning a hole in his brain
tattooing itself on his shoulder. He tries to turn
the translated Russian words into a Texas drawl, camouflaged
in his khaki, slither of a deep scar on his cheek.
Childhood games, Stanley knives slick as tongues.
Now the game is real, guns and words, words and guns
Whose crime whose punishment? End of the day he'll slip
his scorched skin into a cold shower, pop a cool one
dive again into the existential meaning of his actions.

THE ORDINARY UNKNOWN

She gets up in the morning, alarm clock brring brring
grinds the coffee, 3 tablespoons full
brushes her teeth, washes her face.
Long thoughts interrupted by nicotine.

She orders her body into ironed clothes, nothing shows.
Makes her tuna salad, takes her 3 blackcurrant tea bags,
book to read, keys to unlock the office door.
And off she goes down the street wearing her smile, discreet.

Hello, she says to the milkman, the fish brothers, the dry
cleaner, the corner shop. Clip clop go her heels all
the long way to another part of town for not much money.
Routine follows her all the upside down day

typing order into the chaos of other people's lives.
Her fingers never stray from the keyboard.
She frightens no one, no one has bad dreams
imagines spiders, serpents, bananas. There is no message

from the eyes behind the spectacles she wears, the respectable
presentation as Betsy the girl next door, the paperdoll
they call McCall, standing in her apron at the stove,
cooking something for the man she's "little woman" to.

All day music plays on the radio amidst chit chat,
this and that over cups of tea, idle glances at the clock
tick-tock. Time is money running out and night is coming
a footfall away from shadows, wet leaves lurching along the pavement.

What goes on behind those eyes behind the thick glass?
You tell me, she won't. No one sees her late at night
sewing buttons on her torn husband's body, eyes on fire,
rocking, rocking to the same gentle tune all day she's hummed.

SUSPICION

He's jealous of something but he can't find what.
He knows she's in love. Who with? What with?
Her passion is a white hot thing,
it burns through his dreams, her dress.

How can he trust a woman like that?
He looks over his shoulder, under the bed.
He tears through the unread mail
addressed to the woman he fears he doesn't know.

He can't find it between the lines,
can't find it in the address book, in her eyes.
He breaks the lock on her secret box.
What does he find?

A sucking stone, a button, a sea shell.
What can he make of these innocent objects.
Lots, he can make lots out of nothing.
He'll kill her for this, whatever this is.

Stephanie Bowgett

HUSBAND

And then your twisted ring wouldn't stay
on my contracted finger; slipped off with
my clothes to the floor. In the park one day

our tabby-eyed boy, catching April
snowflakes on his tongue, asked me, "Is one
and one the easiest sum in the whole world?"

I didn't dare to speak. Walked through the week
tight-lipped, dodging questions and eyes.
Behind raw lids, I screened the one who changed

with the sky: left me salt-washed, pinned open
pink beyond shame. Wedged cold on my right hand
your ring broke no promises. You didn't

even notice. Familiarity had frozen
two into one, hard. In the thaw I lose
my balance. Night-times, he breathes on my dreams:

I melt. Sometimes I dial his number
hear his voice. Hang up. Sometimes I sit
and write his name   and his name   and his name.

CHINA PLATE

Bent on destruction, white bone stroked giddy,
I ride the spotlight, brittle as sugar.
Up in the air on fear and your fingers,
these breathless seconds were spangled for me.
Stark salt teardrop, spin me translucent. Twist
me up shimmering: plunge me low, catch me.

Smile and bow. They want you to show how close
I came, how dangerous I am. I am.
Drumroll. Applause. Eyes round on you.
You crack me in two. Clean. With gloved hands.

OUTDOOR GIRL

When they did touch, it was always outside, at night.
She would sniff, inhale the cold off his skin,
lick and nuzzle, light-headed with it, breathe in
that smell. Desire shivered, misted ice-bright
eyes. Seamless, outside time, they were held in
black-lace shadows under trees. Released from the dark,
stepping over the sulphur rim of the midnight park
one cool kiss, like brother, like sister. Then he'd be gone.

Kitchen light shines square into her back yard.
She pulls the freezing washing off the line,
buries her face in the chilled folds of a hard
shirt; breathes in   and in   and in,
wraps the sleeves around her neck, tight, tight,
presses her lips to the stiff, white collar.

RUN THROUGH THAT AGAIN

Telescoped with Terry the plumber
in the larder, getting familiar
with my new central heating clock.
Red digits flash. He intones a litany
of manual instructions,
pushes buttons, swears softly

and I am riding outside through
wet blackness, stretched orange light,
one hand on your thigh. You
trace my stockings up; find skin.
We lurch towards the edge,
you jolt the wheel back; grin

and that's the hot water for you.
Terry unfolds, rubs his legs.
"I'm sorry," I say,
"I think I need
to run through that again."

SUNDAYS, HIS WIFE WENT TO SEE HER MOTHER

He'd have her kneel between his knees, stroke
her hair, wild under his hands: would fancy
it was something wild, a squirrel, spitting
vixen, brindled stoat. She would laugh, let him

wash, rinse with infusions of rosemary,
seven jugs of rainwater cold from the
butt. He'd comb coconut oil through its length
burnish to shine with a silk-covered brush.

He wanted to drown in her hair, but it
made his skin burn. *Please Amelia*, as she
stood over him, covering him, *Please*, let
him undo the little buttons she'd sewn

there on purpose. She was one of the tawny
russet kind: hot ginger eyes, those tendrils
round her face, springing like temper, twisting
a man brittle, spent as a matchstick.

Each Monday he'd go home to a flowered
apron, two plain daughters with lank brown plaits
for his dinner of cold mutton and mash:
the white innocent smell of boiling sheets.

Debjani Chatterjee

WORDS BETWEEN US

Language breaks down and sounds have no meaning,
Words splutter, dialogues die in mid air;
You and I cross and there is no meeting.

Eyes do not glance, there is no encounter,
Postures are hidden and gestures are bare;
Language breaks down and sounds have no meaning.

Even masques expose the fading actor,
Curtains are drawn but invite no fanfare.
You and I cross and there is no meeting.

We are less than strangers in theatre,
Playing separate parts in solitaire.
Language breaks down and sounds have no meaning.

Silence replays the role of the jester.
No more are we one, no longer a pair.
You and I cross and there is no meeting.

Too many scenes have started to fester,
Too many pauses are mimes that ensnare.
Language breaks down and sounds have no meaning.
You and I cross and there is no meeting.

HUNGRY GHOST

Today I went shopping with my father
after many years. I felt I was back
in time to when I'd follow grandfather
to the market, smelling the spicy scents,
drinking the sights and mingling with the shouts.
Neither buyer nor seller, I would float
like a restless spirit, hungry for life.

The market is bigger. I have grown too.
There are more goods as distances have shrunk.
The prices are higher. I understand
about money and, alas, its bondage
of buyers and sellers. Almost I wish
I was again that hungry ghost, watchful
and floating through the world's noisy bazaar.

LEARNING THE IMPERIALIST'S LANGUAGE

Because you were the enemy's,
you had to be grappled with
and ruthlessly mastered.
Encountering you was all
the delight of illicit romance.
Analysing you, I discovered
how the enemy thinks.
But this was not enough –
I looked for chinks in the armour;
you gave me the awful
lesson of linking with
what the enemy feels.

No more the enemy's,
you are now mine.
Even the bludgeoning
of rote-learning
brought us together.
You have schooled me
in strategies to disarm,
to rule the enemy with love,
as you have fooled me
into owning at last,
that in possessing you,
I become the one-time enemy.

VISITING E.M. FORSTER

'But Forster doesn't live here any more.'
I knew that of course. He died the year before
– before my passage. I told 'Raised Eyebrows'
that I only wanted... to see his room,
to see the view. Why else would I have come?
'But this is not a museum, you know.'
(Cambridge, not a museum?) I nodded.
'An ordinary room.' Ordinary
is what it takes. I remembered my coach
journey from Canterbury. 'I have come
all the way from India. He was my friend.'
It worked. The brows subsided, defeated.

A bemused stranger occupied the place
– half apologised for everything changed.
The room was functional, anonymous;
he could not have lived here long. 'I'm afraid
even the furniture is not the same.'
What did I care, standing at the window.
Olive groves beside the forget-me-not
Mediterranean rolled below, with
a dust haze veiling the Marabar curves.
'It is the same,' I said, 'nothing has changed.'

Alison Chisholm

AT SOURCE

While you discover dark and wetness,
sound of heart,
my exploration starts in swollen breasts,
sickness, thickened belly.

You find freedom lashing new limbs,
comfort sucking your hand,
rocking as I move. I woman learn
Eve's torment, flood you out,
sever our link.

I inch examine you, strive
to recognise beauty in your red
wrinkled anger. My fingertips
feel coarse against your skin,
scant layered in texture of crocus petals.

You have no use for looking,
mouth trace our bond in milk
nuzzle close to familiar scents.

Our course is set, our journey
charting its way to explore
mazes of tomorrow,
each knowing other better than ourself,
each learning new life.

MAKING SENSE

Talk for twenty minutes
she said.
On what?
I said.
On poetry. Bringing poetry alive
she said.

I thought of poems strapped to operating tables,
electrodes aiming lightning
at their vital parts.
I thought of poems sitting stony faced
while I put on red nose and told them jokes.
I thought of poems itching
under plague of fleas.
I thought of little poems holding hands and dancing
carefree as picnicking teddy bears,
and grown-up poems making love on the living room floor.
I thought of poems beating down
walls of their stanzas, tearing off
tight robes of rhyme, running naked
and free.

Twenty minutes?
I said.
Yes
she said.
And don't try to be clever. Just make sense
she said.

READING PLATH

Words I did not understand dropped sister sounds,
linked subliminal messages. Reading
dissipated hate in me, oiled my rage.

Growing older I became familiar,
caught reason on barbs of truth,
longed to know the mirror's dark side.

I had to travel paths
Electra walked. Shedding scales drew sepia veil
to open new visions stinging with colour.

Now I have learned silence and panic,
see clearly where moonlight corrupts.
Now my eyes are scratched

by blue light, yew branch.
I shut out sight; find images
will not cease shadow play awake, asleep.

AMBER

Gold dangled, a pendulum
swings sunlight, glows.

Tears sapped from tree
or wept by Phaëthon's sisters
petrified to jewelled rock,
trapped frond or insect,
waited.

Today exclamations
note colour, feel texture.
I hold the stone,
stare aeons back to see
honeyed resin solidify.

Its warmth surprises;
pulsing charge shocks.

Rose Flint

SHAMAN

Under the acrid smoke
the dreams were leaping and binding,
trailing their sensuous breath
as watered silk: scarved wolf in the grey,
hackled fox, owl-shadow, secret
oblique lynx; all gathering.

White moon-face, listening slant, she
entices the drum to enter the slender bowl
of her bones; strong thighs
gripping the bucking music,
the rattle of nerves.

To the cage of her flickering wrist
the leopard is called from the shadows.

I swear! her arms grew furred and maculate
as she began the ascension.
Going out with smoke
through the space of the pole star
into the void.

If I lost you
I would sing the drum,
stretch naked for great mottled cats
to inhabit my skin; let my eyes fold inward.
I'd find you, hold:
though the spirits were dancing
the feast of your soul,
I would journey the shallow entrancing skies
with feather bone fire –
bring you back home.

GALLT Y WIDDAN
(HILL OF THE WITCH)

Has she gone into the wary heron
that pleats her great feather cloak
into stillness and stands
wings of slate and her stone headstalk
carefully pivoting, all the awareness
of river's jade, river's citrine,
river's dark quartz
in her black avid eye, kindled blade beak?

Or has she fled gently into the blue smoke
of the bells or the bride-white blackthorn?
(Needlethorns longer than thin fingers,
sharp, dangerous to the heart.)
Is she here in the guise of a fly?
Does she lie in the snake's tight bed
of bracken, or the blue egg
or the spotted snake's head fritillary?
Has she shifted
into the young black bull stamping the juices
from crushed green garlic and wild violets?
Is she crouched in sorrel's white star?

She is here,
speaking under the river's raucous voice:
Listen to me, listen, listen to me...
She is stone, she is water, she is wren,
she is the wind and her breath lifts my hair
as her presence slides over my skin.

THE SWIMMING DREAMS

Falling to sleep through the day's fractures
the slope of your back turned away, white spine
fragile calcined road to a stone Larena;
harsh pallors of sand bury my saying mouth,
stay my hands fretful metronome –
    I am drowning   through dust
    to green water swells,   my dress bells out
and greenwhite legs come frog-open,   float loose
        over reaching river foliage of weeds.
      My shoes kick from my heels and fall   slow twostep
    as snakefish flick my opal skin with little lips
          that kiss and kiss.   I laze
    in the disc of the skirt's rosette; hang fire.

Or when small hours eat the potency of fear
and grow, grin feverish teeth in shadow,
come leaking out of the vulpine pockets, pig-wallets,
the wasp-waist keyholes of the boxes;
when you are hollow, arid weight, stripped mountain –
          then I dream of a chaos of women shining
with water and steam, round deep pool jostling, choppy,
   stones flooded and night air ringing; strong women –
long breasts, otter hair, west sexes tendrilled
    watercress. I dive through the wild mouth, go down
          to the dark trailing peacock cirrus.

Seasons of ash and drought.
We share a delicacy of touch, take infinite care
as we wake our day's landscape: *this is the kingdom*
of today; in the kingdom is a city, in the city
is a garden, in the garden of dry flowers lies a well,
within the liquid well, the dream of kingdom lies.

Other nights of broken sleep and failed desire
the water is nearly breathless. I am fathoms deep,
          horizontal, calm, arms crossed,
   palm to naked shoulder, thighs bound
 down by a cold shell-spiral. Dim spacious sea;

my hair rolls away from me ribboning as black lace,
or blood ebbing slowly away through the tide.

WOMAN WITH A SECRET ROOM

The woman with a secret room
does not speak of it even though her eyes
shine out whichever season, skyblue or
slate-grey gold-flecked they shine out
yet this   is not considered extraordinary,
no one remarks *look at that woman*
how she shines! She must be eating light!
Devouring whole electricity in sparking snakes
between the one negative pole of
her dark finger and the other positive pole of
her radiant day finger, dawn finger, sun finger.
She does not speak of it,
goes about her work, threads the spaces of crowds,
weaving, dancing lets money attend her
like leaves or rain or juggler's pieces;
is hooded as an owl: winter white furred in a tree
of waiting listening bones.
She has a coat like any other coat,
a webbing of thin wools, moorland and heather
mottled there as python   if she spins
in her coat, only the pavement and the stray dog
would attend to her spiral.   *Crazy Mother*
winding her rags, her strings.

The woman with a secret room touches
as delicate as doe, or kitten, her fingertips
charge with love, children cluster, kiss.
Her lover closes his eyes and dreams and smiles –

These her dreams then:
the Wheel and Web Dream, the Dream of Love,
the Tree of Hope Dream, the Dream of Diamond Jaguar,
White Buffalo Woman's Dream. These run over her skin
their feet tattoo her, she is blood and colours,
the dreams prick sharp at her eyes, tears
flood her with water energy, running silk rivers
from her fontanel to her soles.

She has a black and white cat, milk on the step,
firecoal and mornings of old moon paleface
in the fragile sky, opposite weight to the sunrise.
She has a lock of delicate balance,
a key of newborn gold.

Jennie Fontana

CLOSE TO THE SAFE HOUSE

Close to the safe house
and the lake with caged water-lilies
fine ploughing makes the terracotta field
seem soft as spread sheets of washed silk.

But is it a trick of late afternoon light –
the dabs of his sable brush that whisper
an ocean of ripe wheat percussed by rain?
Listen.

Sandy leaf mould trickling
fast as the grains in an hourglass
filling their footprints
between ferns – harebells quivering
as an alert deer's heart.

Can you hear her fingers unhooking
the green bramble thorn
turned through the white of her dress;
the plane flying low overhead;
his father's voice in her dream last night;
the words that must be said?

"THROWING THE LIGHTNESS ON THESE THINGS" *

It is no accident
that tonight as I pull you
from the turned debris of recollection
the baby cries, my daughter vomits –
my son pulls his comforting blanket
closer to his lips.

The last time I saw you
thick fog gauzed a screen between us
leaving the first months
of every year since
tight as TB
caught in my throat.
As the passenger
I had to lean out of the car door
to feel for the kerb in a foreign city
squinting for signs and junctions –
a scarf around my mouth.

•

I clutch my sister
pegging washing on the line.
We go in and watch
fragmented film footage of a forest
deflowered by stretchers and fuselage.

We wait by the Rayburn
for our parents
to come back from their bike ride.
How do you tell your father
his only brother is dead?

At 8 the next morning
the phone call confirming
and his cry
that had me running all the way round
the blind corner

going the long way back to school
where the headmaster sent me home again.

Past the village church
feeding stacks of flame into the sky –
the stained glass cracking
louder than crunched barley sugars.

•

This was not an over-six-foot-box.
I wondered which bits of you they'd got
or if they'd left anything behind
in the forest.
Maybe you were muddled up with someone else –
several people even.
I wondered if they'd arranged you nicely
or just slung everything in.
Perhaps you'd got shifted around on the journey –
all piled up at one end or one side.
Perhaps it was all a mistake
and you weren't there at all,
you'd got lost –
snagged in a tree
and you'd turn up one day
just like you always did
full of exciting new plans:
  "Throwing the Lightness on these things.
  Laughing it all away.
  Laughing it all away."

(*The title of this poem and the last three lines
are taken from Joni Mitchell's *Court & Spark* album.)

DENT IN THE WALL

I

Unmoulded. Barely uncurled. Knew only
the clamp of lips round rubber teat
filling mouth with milk and her own
sounds when cold leaked.
Cries hammered on ear-skins
sealing sharp words – shaping night-space
startling emptiness – arms fight din
reflex shudders – crumple face.
Stuffed with wet wheeling dark
movements rumble swinging light.
Shuddered whites lock the look
up up as if they might...
          wrap and hold
          the limp shell.

II

They never knew the clenched squeal
of laughing body – fists unfolding
as small hands – large hands – feel
the warmth of touch moulding.
Feet dancing on thighs pushing out
the boundaries of a tiny world:
the sucked satin edge of comfort
shredded and discoloured as it's unfurled.
They only knew the numbness
of 'giro' waiting: forty dragging fags a day
and sex,
grudging anything that blocked their way.
A need to make their mark: the unknitted skull
perfectly matched the dent in the wall.

IN HYLANDS PARK

(for Alison)

"I think we scared ourselves," you said
talking on the phone
after husbands had pointed to the clock
and gone to bed.

I remember an owl
hooting once as we headed back.
It feels as if it was every summer night
but it must have been only a handful.

We'd walk as far as the big house
and sit on the steps.
Your open tin between us –
our fingers twiddling rollies.

We'd scratch light after light
with pink tipped Swan Vestas
against the portico pillars.

Reminding ourselves of who we loved
and who was with who;
the ski instructor; Miss Deans and
the field trip to Scotland.

Each flourish was a foothold
as we climbed the wrought-iron gates,
padlocked at sunset,
dropping back into Paradise Road.

AT CARRARA

it was there
Carrara

muffled dynamite

white below buzzing
cheese-wires
that circuit the mountain
to cool

that cut with
sand and water

blocks the size
of buildings
that hold another
David tight

on thin sheets
veined with grey
nuns daily smooth
the surface with their soft shoes
and hard prayers

minister the sick
hold the pain

my great aunt
and her reputation
in pink pyjamas
unperturbed by death
and charity

she twitched like the
taut wire
boyfriends on her lips
with cock-eyed lipstick

she'd buzzed round
mountains all her life
blasting holes
in her passport
so they wouldn't
guess her age

no marble angel
at her head
just jewels
and property
that passed through other hands
like rosaries

each diamond
each pearl
each brick
each lover
uttered by
relatives and
set into crevices
and wired
with a long fuse

Linda France

IF THIS IS SPRING

"I want to call this, *life*"   Adrienne Rich

I.

Giving birth to itself   is something new
crying in the night   Shock
of breathing   air like fire   black-paper wings
of words   like *trust*   *surrender*

The smell of fledgling trust   is skin
you ache to touch   woven bone
and follicle   a rope of feathers   stretched
between you   hand to hand
feeling   the pull   of air

If someone opens the door too wide   everything
will kindle   into flame   and bone
will be nothing   but a charred cage
Christen it *maybe*   *hazard*

II

Over hacked hawthorn   anonymous birds
are trilling   their tea-tray racket   Light
is pouring   molten silver   I know
this road   like the map   I carry
mined   from the contours of my palm

Anything new is a surprise   beachcomber's eye
tuned to different notes   counterpoint
So the stark white sign   propped on prongs
of ripped twigs   like a lectern   slashes
the silence   with its desire   for   QUIET

drowns the instinct of birds   seasons
the roar it stirs   in me   walking past

and back again   unable to find it   heed it
Singing like a bird   quietly   out loud   is what
I dream of   the impossible   becoming invisible

III

South is shelter   two in a field   wide-eyed
as aconites   leaning into the scent of milk
lanolin   testing the elbow of separation
legs   not-yet-able to stand   on their own
feet   two greedy mouths suckling

I am a needle   threaded with grey   stitching
more than miles   dizzy   with this new
geography   my inclinations   Wind constant
as a friend   as breathing   the ridged fleece
of borrowed socks   my boots full of knots

Then   time shirrs   and it's one wing   beating
a bell in the north   ringing out rain
to wash thought away   wind unravelling green
dreaming to be born   I learn
again   to say   *lambing storm*

IV

Wild garlic   is green tongues   hot sharp ribbons
tying the wood   in shiny bows   How many
is two   Your mouth   chewing   You don't know
anymore   who   it belongs to   Lips fraying

like curled chrysantheums   The sound of your voice
cracking   like a new egg   gold in a bowl
sticky with something raw   Its eyes staring   you down
Its quickfire I I I   Its many and tedious deaths
If this is life   you want to call it STOP

And still all your little lambs   come home   You count
their tails   like ladybird spots   saved
from the fire   Black dots   before your eyes
red from smoke   weeping

V

Spring is dying from too much wishing
breaking out in an adrenalin sweat
shivering yellowing pinned down by the weight
of sky showers of sharp rain

If this is Spring it's tender afraid
to open its stillborn eyes I can only listen
for the sound of skin tearing its first
beautiful words telling me how to grow

A WOMAN CALLED NORTHUMBERLAND

What I am is an acknowledged land
of changing borders, rivers that curl

like hairs left on pillows, hills
rising and rolling, the limits of skin

that won't stay still. And what I am
is roaring, a bull being itself,

leaving hoof prints in stone, cups
and rings filled with honey and sweat.

The land I am made of stone
and growing things touches the sky,

the fresh inevitable air of weather.
We talk to each other and decide

on the best thing, milk each other's
goodness into silver jugs I fill

with lilies and arrange on altars
where I make no sacrifices not mine

alone; only the sound of stone
softly roaring, the invisible breath

of bread rising, an acknowledged land.

SONG FOR THE PLACE OF THE CATTLE

First thing and last thing we know no borders.
What we are is the grace of a warrior
thinking about the colour of moon

on water, waiting for a dream to come true
like day. And when exactly does dawn begin?
Water is spilled, a bloodied dew, on earth

and the twined rope of flesh is cut so skin
against skin is milk flowing, tears falling,
bread breaking. We feel our bodies grow,

like oak, into crosses we carry; bark
thickens into the limits of one against one,
the north and south of escaping horizons.

With every new day we forget the name
of the borderland is love, the threshold:
and can't stop crying. May the memory

return, as acorns do, chalices stored
against the ache of winter. May autumn
be another door opening onto

the gift of a single good, everything
between first and last. Sweep your body
over the sill and let the song of wind

and weather stir your branches. Feel your eyes
open like buds and watch the way your sky
can dance in miraculous shades of blue.

HOME COOKING

It was usually at the tea-table
that my mother dished out her small morsels
of advice with the dangerous brown pie
and drowned opal cabbage, knives and forks passed
on by my grandmother, fat mugs of tea
the colour of Italian hillsides:
a setting forever coupled with *sex,*
religion and politics – three taboos
not to be mentioned by a modest girl
in mixed company. I think it saved her
from forming an opinion
apart from *No.* I said *Yes* to all three
and more than one permutation. Another thing
she was fond of saying: *You think too much*
– it'll only end in tears. Wise woman;
despite herself. Politics, religion
and sex – three things certain to end in tears.

Sarah Hopkins

IN PASSING

it looked as if a mechanic
had hung himself, but it was just
his boilersuit fat with wind
bellowing on the line

he was probably quite a thin man
being sensible somewhere else,
careful not to blow himself up,
keeping the door shut, unperturbed

but what of his wife at the window
who'd pegged him in this boisterous wind,
was it for her like having him there
buffeted, spun and speechless?

LOOKING IN

oh for a quiet table
set with salt and pepper
in little pots

and not this
reckless seasoning
out where wind never stops

MAD MARGARET

She is a blue tit
blue-lipped, blue
unlit bit
staring on a hairy day
of breeding weeds
feathers of her face
sweating
beetles in her eyes
sharpening themselves
for a piece of peace
of an unsmelled hill

'...there is a green hill far away...'

there she is, bobbing up
and down now
pecking at the fog
perched and earthed
on raw oaken knees
that do not bend
without sedation

'...a green hill...'

nose dribs and drabs
down flat-chested
twin-set and
furry old spittle
flies out
all her mutterings

'...far away...'

and there she is again
bobbing up and down
wringing wooly hem
all moustache and twigs
and coils of hair
there: years and stones

from the unsmelled hill
face eyes mouth
ticking tocking
like some damned
discarded clockwork bird
whose every booming
wound-up second
hurts.

THE BOOK

On your head
put it right on your head

you limping girl
who can't walk good.

See now, how you straighten
if you try.

See now, you're like a queen.

No-one would know it was you.

ON BEING A STAR

We five-pointeds, torn from light
unshepherded, kinked, spoked and spat
recall exotic origins in order to survive.

Hear us fall to earth bereft of sight
pulled down to dress in leaves and hats
we five-pointeds, torn from light.

All are stardust, yet we fail what might
in towns so far off heaven's track
recall exotic origins. In order to survive

we try the way unbraided, forgetting, half-alive
busy with pointlessness, making do on fat
we five-pointeds. Torn from light

stardom mocks; the glamour is unright.
Yet such artificial moments, when order cracks,
recall exotic origins in order to survive.

Arms, legs and heads will not suffice
to struggle with what gravity would snatch.
We five-pointeds, torn from light,
recall exotic origins in order to survive.

Libby Houston

OUT OF REACH

Cabin lights, deck lights, navigation lights
keep back the stars

A corner where the wind
had sent a drift of brown petals
as if the boat had left some river-mooring

Waving from the rail
or leaning on the rail or throwing
the quick snow of a torn note at the gulls

A body that was found
on the grey sand near the campsite
its anonymity sealed like a stone

The drive to Inverness in a black sack
further still

TRIPPING OVER THE SAME OLD SUNSET

A crimson lollipop: he licked it.
A new world solemnly rose into orbit
like a great balloon.
                    It was, and he pricked it.

A LITTLE TREACHERY

From this turn in the path, look –
that web of twigs is the last,
the last skin if you like.
Beyond that, the sky's bare.
Whatever. Don't be afraid.

When we step into the full light,
all your woodland skills then suddenly
useless as fishes' gills for air,
the worst thing is regret – don't let it in,
don't give it ground enough
for a fly's egg.

All this, these, clotted stacks of leaves,
ramson aroma, the colourless flowers you love,
hairgrass like fountains, saturated mould,
steep cries, dry wings, fern plumes, the nightingale,
green tripwires, freckles of light, rot-muffled falls,
this blinkered scope, soft, sharp, partitioned, still –
feast on the old familiar, imprint if you want, now.
We don't come back. You know that – and the stories,
no looking back.

We say goodbye to it once just.
Then. Not yet. Once, at the edge, where
what's beyond – no one's said more than that.
Except – and I'm sure it's true –
nothing to fear. Except, to start at least,
we walk arms wide, palms open.

So, the cargo you've picked up, the significant cones,
the eggshells, mousebone, beakbone, flowers, stones,
leave. There, at the edge. Like an offering
at the gate. You're shivering.

Don't be afraid.
I can go first, if you like, into the bright space.

I shall be walking backwards reading your face.

BICYCLING TO THE BRIDGE ON A RAINY EVENING

west's rain in the face:
when I turn home I'll be done
on both sides, like toast

NOTES FROM AN AUTUMN JOURNEY

The sun spreads her exaggerated gestures
over the vast screen home
like a mother left behind
to her Italian wine and chiffon
in the mirror by the telephone.

Offside window-seat on the westbound coach
I could have spent the whole journey looking down
on *laps*, the laps that were passing us in the fast lane
in an unexpected succession of vulnerability

Well, being carried past – the passiveness
of passengers, these passers, passagers,
no one even holding food or a book, or map. My angle
bows their heads down for them – how they look humble

Because it's a view more usually of small children
told to behave, sit still? Or en masse the pose
of a congregation below the pulpit, a concert audience, yes
from the gallery: *demure*. And I am aware

of shying away from the poignancy of fast lives,
their likely certainty, confirmed by each heartbeat,
of the body's immortality

a whiplash can crack – Each of these lives
hangs in the hands of a driver (out of my line of vision),
each one consigned with no other rite than the belt click
to mark an act solemn and common as love's

And mine. And so does mine. And of turning more easily
to the video's old screams and bullets,

explosions, blood and scrap. By now her frowsy
wraps awry, the sun is bowed
to follow her headache to bed, the wine in the end
won out – and yet their folds are rich
with hint enough of an immutable grandeur
millennia in the gutter could not alter.

Rabbit-time, but not this side.
A fox on the outward run this morning
smeared, still wet, near the central reservation,
somewhere, Wiltshire – what would be left of it
now?

The letters from friends that I brought I let
carry me off, fast, light, spun like the turns of a
game to a Pennine terrace, a flat in Denmark,
a Tiverton attic, a hilltop, I think, in France – addresses
whose doors have no height or colour for me yet,
under the night already, or the coming night. Friends,

poets. And myself, then, I think:
we have all been touched by the blast,
scarred or infected, the real touch of the Muse I mean,
faltered, lost our footing

Certainly gave up, not realizing
surrender was never accepted, left unopened –
not till the next impassable next trap next chasm
and we were giving up again, giving in. And so on.
Giving another word. And who am I speaking
for?

Nothing stops, nothing has stopped.

Lucently white, fish-white and quivering
the video in reflection hangs high to the right ahead
right on the sultry cloud. In real perspective there's
Clint Eastwood, *Harry*, going on before
into the real sunset

This is really the exit.
Arrival eye-level, point-blank, all directions.

Louise Hudson

VIDEO

Watching this film
I am the woman,
the man is you.
He has her
in his hands,
I forget how they'd come
together.
I drink
let the beer
slip
cool in my throat
it stings
so that my eyes water.
Time for another can
I pull the ring
it spurts into my face
and the couple
uncouple
breathing fast.
I sip slowly.
They cannot stop
kissing, making love
it sounds
too good
to be true.
I gulp my drink
and close my eyes
to the screen.
Soon it will be time
for another drink
I flick through channels
lick froth from my lips;
the glass is empty
and mucky from the foam.

I try to concentrate
on the story line.
Their story's not like mine
she doesn't mind
being with him
that much.
They touch each other
in ways that make me
grab another can
who needs it anyway
I switch off
wash my glass
pretend to sleep
alone.

FOR LOU REED

I am a woman who walks alone
and I love it
don't want to be sidetracked
down streets of desire
where shop windows light up
at the mere sight of him.
I want to be able to skip
to the part of town
where the men who've let me down
can be seen, inside their 2-bed homes,
on summer nights,
drying up in those funny aprons
with tits and tassles.
No more hassles about when he'll phone
they've all gone public.
I walk away from suburb safety
now the only men I meet
are from the street
and I don't care if they want me,
then, there,
it's better than town planning
everything neat and in its place.
After, they can drift to their next meeting
love has no place here, has to keep moving
there are no pitches left
they've all been taken by people who sell.
The kids think "poor cow
can't find anyone to love
to love her"
but oh I can
anytime, anywhere,
when I want
only
I like it, here, alone on the street
keep on walking
feet.

OPEN TOP

Thinking about you
and sex
I drive too fast
down country lanes.
Driving barefoot
is like dancing
with no knickers
it feels so good.
Your voice breathes
against my neck:
I come to a stop.
The engine's ticking over
and I am breathless
with the sound of a bass
guitar.
I do not think
how far it can go
but cruise with you
alone.
Nothing to lose
and nothing much to gain
except delight at speed
and a reckless wish
for light and air.

COUNTING THE DAYS

Again
Blood
mucking up her plans
damning her with its constancy.
Each time it is the same
she tries to ignore the pains,
the cramps,
pretends this time there is a
taste
different
skin
different
everything
different
but
again
there is blood
it slimes its way down
like sperm
leaving her body
the same.
Sex is a bore now
a chore
a means to a beginning
determined by ringed days
and she counts
as he enters
odd it will be a boy
even, girl.
He's already got kids
says it doesn't matter
but it matters
each time the blood
comes
snide as that woman
his wife
who had hoards of them
and didn't want them.
It will be different soon

she will not drop
her babies as blood
but carry them carefully
take care.
She's read so many books
knows what they will be like
at each week
when there will be toes,
eyes,
hair.
By six weeks
it is a pip:
she cannot cut
into fruit now
but sucks on it
tonguing the seeds
until she spits them out.
This time her baby stains
the pad
red tears slide
indifferent, steady, rhythmic
next time, next time
it will be different
and she will never be
the same.

Judith Kazantzis

TO LOST EVE

Because I can't salt your tail
or send you even a naked Adam singing
It's moi, cheri, on the doorstep
nor string two silver words to
say your Pope Joan, tell your Widow of Bath,
your Clytemnestra, your Cleopatra,
the beads of the rosary of your beauty –

All the more
shall I pray for acceptance
after the fall, of your imperfect proverb
(an incoming call, fragmented, someone
called Eve, strange, I think it's you.
Definitely I'll accept it!)

One silver pear in my hand,
worth all the golden apples hanging
perfectly on the tree.

EYE

Every bird sang,
only in her eye
every bird dressed
in a pinafore of ice.
Their feathers danced
like ice-floes.
Their eyes hip-hopped
like fish roe.
It seemed in her eye only,
not the general view,
some tuck
to the cornea
that puckered the lens,
some tic of birth
for which her mother screamed
and had her skew-eyed.
No, not a squint,
she didn't wander,
she kept intact
as a winter hawk.
Its talons glued to the bark,
all winter
it trained its frozen eye
on a frozen fountain
of dancing balls of feathers:
for one day
there would come
from under the raised water's stare,
deeper down,

a translation,
a wave of voices crying
in her own tongue.

NIGHT

When the traffic went home
night walked up and down the pavement,
bitterly cold, blowing on its fingers.
I leaned out of the window, calling, 'Night!
Come in. I will warm you under my duvet,
that flock of silk
as warm as your mother's thighs.'

But night didn't look up, it walked by,
blowing bitterly on its knuckles,
muttering and grumbling. 'What are you muttering
about, excuse me,' I asked. Night said
not a thing, but as the moon sank,
the birds intervened and the leaves
lightened their colour to green.

When night sank away,
then, followed by crowds, came driving
broad and palpable day
down the length of my road,
at first whistling courteously under the leaves,
then barreling, revving, thundering,
till my windows sprang to with attention,

and as night sank slowly away,
so does my duvet of silk
sink off my bare bones.

TOWARDS MORNING, KEY WEST

Rain sounds out the wood and tin
in a matter of seconds,

elucidates the outline thoroughly,
makes a mouth-organ:

wood walls, tin roof, porch,
slinking, banging, creaking, patting.

You and I in parallel
lightly are breathing bedfellows

inside this water and house patter,
inside this long elucidation.

I think it's a hundred quiet years
since we kissed and fell asleep.

LOOKING THROUGH THE ALBUM

1

And now this is my mother
who bore me and others
whose love, or is it my love for her,
blanches me continually,

an almond in a pan,
whiteskin, peeled, without a hide.

Nothing, I've got nothing to declare!
– But what a nonsensical fear.

My gallant mother strongly smiling,
white hair blown back out of curl,
in the terse and ferocious wind
your cheeks are always
indisputable roses.

2

Out of the powerful sky
we caught the white snow falling,
when we were seven; then we
palmed it, built it and fired it.

Turning from the sky's purity
we killed each other,
employing some thumping ballgames you'd
say calmly never were; yes but
we were thumping like creatures mating,
yet we never were.

How shining are your eyes
inside this snowy-margined print.

Minnows in a pot,
wriggling pottage.
The bag of worms I had to trot

and bring for the goldfish,
their slime three-legged in each other,
pink, claret,
guts for angel-fishes' garters,
a skinny jostle,
Armageddon at the moving core.

Heat of constant irritant.
The pan smokes with freezing fire.
Disturbance!
Call the engines! Call the engines!

Nestling in the space left, hollow
of the living sphere, flies and fruit,
the best I could make.
But every day and dawn and evening
where were you? I had
such childish questions.
The wind has dropped, the sun's come out.

3

Your authoratative picture reigns here,
tranquillity of the cleared sky,
to be guarded, marvelled at,
a miracle proclaims its rosiness,
a draught of goldfishes,
a perfectly white avalanche of milk
might be expected any moment
if I never look away.

How shining grow your eyes.

4

Using her mask,
her wormy eye-holes,
now listen to an old child's
papery prayer:
Put your smile in the cupboard,

for I'm not here,
Don't lap up all my skim of goodness
and scour me out of answering smiles.
– I'm not here.
(How rose and snow unite in you.)
Don't set me in the pan any more,
don't skim me alive
on the fire of my love any more.

Little keeper of the roses,
indisputable and ferocious roses.
Not here. Not here.
Let us end this papery prayer,
let us close the book of smiles.

MY DADA

Arguing liberation theology
with my Dada, who still prefers the divine
forefinger of the wholly furious Papa –
there comes a warm loud wumph over and above
the sunwarmed serpentine brick wall, and the white-
breasted cat loitering among the lilies
flees, one paw suspended first on the moss
– And again a higher, departing wumph – I
cry, Dada, look up, and there in the sky, flies
higher and higher a circus in the blue air:
red, blue and marigold yellow, a Big Top –
a balloon, rising with stately soft starts
of ignited gas, the fire at the top of heaven,
the Holy Fire on our blessed brows,
danced by the south west wind across
the peach and the plum trees, and kept lit by
three Victorian gentlemen, whose faint black
top-hats grow hazier and higher. *Ora pro*
nobis, they begin to call down in Latin
but when last heard they're shouting: *Viva, Viva,*
Compañeros, Viva! and *No Passeran!*
And down between rose and lily, nervous cat
and wall, there come twirling three hats in one style,
three white sombreros. One my Dada wears now
and one I wear and one the small cat dreams in,
her nose alternately twitching with her tail.

Mary Maher

EASTER SUNDAY

She took
her kite to the park
and forgot to climb
the man on the horse
put her arm around his cold neck
after she'd rubbed off
pigeon crap.

She only
had eyes for the sky
and then string caught around
the man's neck
before the yellow bird
singling out the ground
plummetted at her feet.

BRIDGES

A group of women walkers
from our village
are up in the air.

Joy, for whom we're sad,
has lost her man
and in his memory planted

a cherry tree
on Lanacre Bridge.
Lanacre is where our walks begin,

where later we take off
our boots to paddle
and cool down.

Gorse and mountain ash
grow naturally at Lanacre,
not cherries, Vera says

who's trying to forget
a man she met at Lanacre.
And what she did.

IVY...

we have your
garden dibber, black
umbrella, brown
hobnail boots, still
with mud on. We
haven't cleaned them.
They're hanging
in the stable where
your mother housed your
trap and pony.
Pannier market's
still on Thursdays.

Nellie from over
Ambow, said
your father had
clappers to frighten
birds in the cherry
tree. We have found
those; hand hewn
and woodwormed.
And the butcher's stones
used for weighing meat
after slaughter
at the farm.
Rounded heavy river bottoms
with a flat side from the bed.
We've found two – a rough
XXIIII is cut
into one and it does
weigh 24lbs. Another
marked H weighs
half a stone.

Nellie said she sat
in the old hearth
on a three-legged
easy tipper,
(in case the cow kicked)

and looked up the chimney to the sky
when she was seven.
She died four years ago
when she was seventy three.
Four years after you.
She gave us a photo
of you; blurred
in a long bathing
costume. We've made
a pewter frame.

BEING ASKED BY MICHAEL

The coalman came
every other Friday.
This was his last visit.
I was moving.

He'd seen me warm,
filled the bunker up
when I wasn't there, never pushed
when I hadn't much money.

A poor speller in the village
leaves money out *For The Coolman*.
Coal dust gleams
in the whites of his eyes.

We shook hands.
'How's your poetry?'
How did he know? I'd never said.
I opened up a packing case

and gave him a *Snowfruit*.
'I'm called a lot of things,'
he smiled, 'but could you write
To Michael in it?'

I don't think he really expected
an answer to his original question.
He wouldn't have had
the time to wait anyway

but eventually it came,
'Very well, thank you.'

KEEPING THEM IN THEIR PLACE

He gave her
the red bound atlas
usually kept
on his passenger seat
with instructions of how
to join him
at his favourite spot.

Flicking
through the counties
in the motorway cafe
she touched on a letter
with a route
in minute detail
to Ruth in Kent,

a rough sketch
and note
from Rachael,
on the North Yorkshire Moors
'I'll have a hot meal,
ditto welcome
waiting.'

Beth
from Middlesex
couldn't wait
to put flesh and blood
to his voice,
'Fork right
then park further up.'

That Friday night
found
pieces of ripped map
– birdsize –
flying all over Gloucestershire.

Val Pancucci

A MAN OF CAUTION

He painted the wood with creosote
sealed up the flight holes
sat up all night
thought he could hear
                    the clicking of jaws
deep in the timber
stood guard with the
                    aerosol can
finger poised
but found each morning
                    (just the same)
a heap of sawdust
on the floor.

He bought a dog
one of the savage kind
trained it in his way
                    to sit and stay
attack on command
to guard his house
                    his wife
all those things that
                    (In a manner of speaking)
made up his life
but after dark
when footsteps were heard on the stair
fangs drawn, hackles raised
its breath traced channels of fear on
the cold window pane
even though
                    (it was plain to see)
no one was there.

He bought a lock

fixed a chain
drilled a spy-hole
in the broad wood door
through which
alarm primed
bolt shot
he now stands
      squinting
into the fish-eye distance
sees the path empty
the far gate closed
under a lilac sky

yet

out of the corner of his eye
detects a sly grin
sees a shadow brush
the cuneiform steps where
      (someone) stands
waiting to be let in
      while

upstairs
under the crumpled sheet
his wife cries out
      (a name)
in her sleep.

ROSAMUNDA

THIS Bay
articulates a natural
boundary
half-hexagon yard
of rampant growth
latin tags intact
curvaceous Lipstick Vine
nuzzles Maiden
hair
sudden lust
in Blushing Bromeliad
generates overspill
IT WILL ALL END IN
Baby's Tears
adapted she
languishes
cultivates stigmata
dim
lit under
MIND YOUR OWN BUSINESS
floppy parasol
fronds by Parlour Palm
slashed patina of Cheese Plant
dispossessed a raving Yucca
constant the kettle clogs
aggravated stomata
GIVE HER AIR
mass transportation
vaporous a sigh rises
threads
macrame noose mesh
she tends to
epical failures
fractured capillaries
CHRONIC oedema
in a Crown of Thorns
behind/her head/repeated
puffball patterns
sequential in the nets

belie

THE THEME

below
the south
grinds circular
PAST

STILL LIFE

defines movement
in an absence
impaled vitality
to convene geometry
                on a table
a shadow casts an apple
encounters residual paradox
a blade
pivots on the parameters
points to/severed neck
     of a refracted guitar
dedication to trivia
the compote on the interchange
decides the question
of a bruised pear
     on the jagged interface
a slice of life
                BURIED ALIVE
from the tabloids
cut & paste text
distorts received signs
an autistic convention
                ARRESTED decay
labours to deconstruct
     HANGING liquescent cloth
extends the downward trend
                A LIFE SENTENCE
vintage aqua vitae
skull & dried flowers
scattered seeds
'exquisite corpses'
subtitled
NATURE MORTE.

THE ROSE

i

In hands soiled
from cropping cabbages
you bring me a rose
torn from your garden.

ii

In the centre
is a seed of moisture
by midnight
the rose is full-blown
where is my mind's spying-glass now?

iii

I wear the rose in my hair
to please you
clusters of leaves
conceal a thorn
three beads of blood
stand out on my forehead.

iv

Our mouths touch half-open
the musk of dead roses
passes between us.

v

I stand naked before my mirror
look for a child
in the speckled dusty glass
the rose branch
brushes against the windowpane.

vi

Stillborn
the rose with a canker
at its heart
never unfolds.

vii

The moon gapes aflame
in the glass the rose
seeps from petals to stem
stains the water blood-red.

viii

High in the holly tree
a rose blooms
among the dark spears
bold usurper
where no berries are.

ix

Polar white
the sun burns a hole
in the skin of the night
scars a heart scoured clean.

x

In the morning
I find a heap of petals
on the pillow.

Joan Poulson

ENGLAND, DECEMBER

The sun hangs low, cleft pomegranate,
her ripeness pagan on this grayling day.

Strange fish, they need temperatures
of below six degrees
before they can be sexually active.

Your preference is for heat,
scorching days on the Coromandal Coast,
English evenings of heatwave
when the melting scents
of philadelphus and stock
are seductive as fingertips.

Now the mist ghosts out the landscape,
the frost's appeal diminishing
as the temperature drops
as the crisp whiteness loses definition.

DAUGHTER

He's back digging graves,
feet rain-sloshing,

nothing but water
and the sound of his spade
biting earth.

She said he'd abused her.

On the windows raindrops
ping......
timing every centimetre
he digs out;
time it's taken
for her to become sixteen.

HEAD COVERING

I have to wear
so many hats these days
he said

that I've started
to lose them

and the wind blows
cold on my brain

and the sun burns
scorches
the inside of my head
melts my mind

rain
has filled up
all the crevices

it's beginning
to overflow

but it's alright
      nobody
knows

and if they ever notice
they just think
I'm crying.

COMING TO TERMS

The blackbird draws her
outside

she's always said
they'll live in the country
together, some day

Yesterday she'd scarcely
recognised him,
yellow tissue paper man.

A pine bonsai, grown from
seed, flaunts full-sized needles

in the hills, she'd planned
where they'd always ended-up
on rides in her childhood

She plucks
at the pine needles,
ripping away excessive energy.

It's possible to let go
a dream; this other too sudden,
she isn't ready, tries to negotiate
one more summer......

A door slams
ends the blackbird's song;
he lifts, flies,
black on grey

the sky never quite clear
in the city.

Possibilities......
fearful, impossible;
she discards
attempts to gain time

stares down
into her hand.

In the yard there's a patch
of mossy grass; she scatters
the pine needles
broadcast in brief flight.

On her fingers
invigorating scent
of the hills.

Wendy Richmond

THE WAY OF IT

Sometimes there's a sax sweating of the earth mined jewel,
and the men herded to labour for the sparkle.
But our land has brass bands trumpeting the end
of a pit, the coal dust settling into the mud.
    My sister writes to me of home
    where the fields sag over the seams
    gutting the ground, like a mattress.
Sometimes there's a coil of white cloud pulling my eyes
off the gutter and into the just blue.
    My sister asks for a reply
    repeating that He will forgive
    all again and again, and more.
Sometimes it's the way the blade of the knife gouges
out the potatoe's eye, slices chips in the palm.
    My sister tells of mother's apron,
    the way of the wiping of her hands.
    She has stopped dying her hair.
Sometimes it's a knitting pattern, red polo-neck
with large snowflakes, sometimes a painted metal bucket
and books always books and the red lipstick.
Most times it's the sweat of the sax.

VOW

I'm trying to lose things, putting them places
where they'll get picked up, turned around
found in oddments til one day they'll just go
like his final rift – "A certain sense of loss."

His first foothold was a repeated onslaught
on my heart, love, I love, I love you. Too
much emphasis on a phrase. Pricing the time
he took my diary and my diet and I slept badly.

My capacity to give gave way. In my sickness
and his current health I want only to hear
he can't concentrate, has reddened eyes,
won't talk and eats rice pudding from the tin.

THE ISSUE HERE IS CONSOLATION

A wasp circled the raspberry jam between us
I flinched when you squashed it with the back
of the spoon as you explained about special saints.
I could come to Mass, you'd have to check on the priest
but sure! I took a photo, you in the foreground
of roses and white railings. I stopped taking pictures
as it hit me that you did believe in a powerful being
and ritual and meaning. I hung onto questions
and even apologised for my doubt. Yes,
it's absolutely right about shadows and daylight
coming from one side leading you to believe
in a totality about the background.
But walking back I began to merge into the trees
I took my time knowing you had somewhere to go.
Back at the caravan I sponged the blood-stained cover
I had to get on with it but it wouldn't go back
the way it used to be and after white wine I rocked
my arms cradling the mistake.

DIARY

Tuesday
Second time in six days I'm talking erotica
in the break with a man I don't fancy.
Wednesday
My womb drags into an ache. I make
the students sit one desk apart.
Thursday
Shout at daughter for wearing my knickers
says she got sent out of science because of me.
Friday
Mistook for a woman I don't like anymore
decline second glass of wine. leave early.
Saturday
Man from Tuesday rings to thank me
for something I haven't done. Talk hangs.

YOUR FATHER

He flattened his curls with Brylcream and made
a play of his Christmas Old Spice stinging –

all father, my dad. After my first checked
bra she warned me not to wear just my blue

nylon nightie – he didn't like it. That
and the tight ribbed polo and mini. Man

of all trades, Jack (never the lad), lost his
rag often as I tried to get thinner

than Twiggy and a single apple was
too much and my eyes did not sparkle.

I loathed the tyranny of his mood and
her silent coalescence. I went out

with any boy who asked – having one was
preferable, liking him was never the point,

being part of something, being his girl
was. Love? No! More of a map reference.

Susan Sheppard

FROM WHERE THE BIRD FLEW

Indigo Buntings tussle in the pine.
There's the shell of a cloud with a broken shoulder
heading west. This screened-in porch, which admits ghosts,
is bearded with wasps. My foot is a rose boat
floating off, off into black and wild ferns.
I am sad and there is no reason.
Each July is filled with tigers,
the talc of the road dusting their faces.
Each July the crow splits the green
and disappears into a sky of sawdust.
I dreamed last night you said *no*
and your finger pointed me
in another direction. That yonder tree is blue
and the tree beyond it is even bluer, until the tree
outside this distance is quite beyond color, just as the light
inside your skull is neither blue nor kind, nor
has it ever been. The other day
under the impatiens, a robin's egg
hammered by the rain to a blue, gritty powder.
I remember the one pale eye which caught my eye,
how behind it there was the intrigue of shadows,
that secret place from where the bird flew
and carried your thoughts to mine.

INTO THE VISIBLE WORLD

for Scarlet Elisabeth
born April 23, 1991

And so, you swam from me
whistling like a porpoise, your rose-grey skin
gleaming, its salt under my mouth which held fast
as a barnacle. I noted the tiny grubs

of your hands, the evidence of your beauty
plain as the hair of fine kelp, hair smoky and black
as undersea caverns. And so, they placed you

between my knees, that drape of seasick green,
the swarm of harsh lights and strangers talking.
Yet there was the strong knotted cord I alone

had cast which dragged you into the visible world.
They snipped it away like a girl's long braid.
I can only say this. I fell asleep.
I awoke another person.

It was then my love for you became a stream
examining itself, its waters rushing through
like silk and leaving the body empty.

FOR MY UNCLE WHO DIED BY HIS OWN HAND

It was raining a pale urine that day.
The leaves of brown scabs opened slowly
into green flames. A crown
of tiny blue flowers erupted in the thorns
and a wren tore open her breast
just trying to escape.

You were up again, your eyes creamy
and dark from all-night brooding.
You sat on the hillside with your rifle,
its wood a lavish coffin you polished everyday.
You saw the sun wake up with a wrinkled forehead
and the lights turning on in the houses one by one.

So you rationed out the bullets. You loaded up the gun.

A king on a throne of mossy rocks,
you watched your life spill into a valley
of shacks with glistening tarpaper roofs
and coal smoke teeming in the tops of trees.

You thought of the poor
with their eyes of yellow fat,
all of the women you loved and feared.

A hawk circled you and screamed,
making its wreath of mercy above your head.
The winds stopped in a sudden hush.
You felt the trigger of your heart jam.
You listened to your chest tear.

The wind lifted then skirted like a bride
down the aisle of russet fields. You put the cold,
familiar ache of the barrel to your lips.
Things has never been more clear.

THE WINTER MOTHER TRIED TO LEAVE

Even before, my parents had filed themselves away.
There were long spaces in the house, terrible
drafts of *something* being held in.
Everything was cold and lousy then.

The tattered curtain blew.
The roof groaned under packed pockets
of deep snow. At the end of the yard,
winter trees huddled into glistening nests.
My father stayed in bed, but
he kept disappearing, sinking
into the mattress, like a body covered
with the gunpowder of dead leaves.

Someone had taken the phone away.
There was only lard and sugar in the cupboard.
I think it must have been Christmas,
or shortly thereafter, that my mother stood
in front of the bathroom mirror as if
it were a high church window
lighting up her face.
She took the small-bristled brush
and extended one sable eyebrow into her temple.
A sharp wing lifted from the side of her face.

Whoever it was coming to save her
never showed that day. And so, the flung
shutters of her heart closed with the same
metallic finality of a jailhouse door.

After that, my mother never leaned
to kiss us. We never asked her to stay.
Now I know when something holds you fast,
you must unbar the door, you must find a way.

WHEN THE DOOR OPENED

The day my father died
the wind knocked the fire out
in the house. We sat around in our coats
staring at the floor.

Hours before, they carried my father out,
eyes frozen open, hand clutched
over the still nugget of his heart.
Everything else in the world kept moving.

In the kitchen, dishes were stacked
where my father had earlier placed them.
The hills swam up like a sickness.
Birds flew over like stray bullets.

My brother sat on our father's unmade bed
clasping his elbows and shaking
his boot. I floated from room to room
as invisible and unnecessary as oxygen

remembering the last time I saw my father
he was sitting small on the blue sofa
with the gold fire of a cigarette
burning close to his knuckles. I hesitated.

See you, I said and looked back
at him staring clean and sober
out of pale eyes. When finally
the door opened, something cool
and swift moved through me.

A month later,
we sat on the shelf of his grave
listening to outsiders talk,
stiff in pressed clothes
and shiny shoes made of coffins.

I could not look at my father,
nostrils pinched into the long drip

of a miner's candle, hands folded
over his chest like linen.

Instead, I watched a lilac wisp
flower up in the distant timber.

I could only think of the red coal
of his brain gone out, the worn blue
shawls of his eyes closed forever. My father
lying there in the casket, I could only
think of his poor, indescribable life.

Penelope Shuttle

SOME RIVERS

Gave me some rivers some moons some rain, I forget when
Gave me all sorts of things, darker things, shames and limbos,
took them, had some
stars rushing overhead, their molten lives they have, forget all that
and what clouds at night like tiny floating needles through blue
and who was it taught me to wear silk and live in a civilized manner,
I forget

Given things, like blue which is the colour that wants
to be every other colour at once

Who paints hands on my door? Who has some rivers? Some things? Some
hands painting some hands on some doors?
Who has some stars? Some rain? Some clouds at night? Some biscuits?
Am I holding some unhurt hands some rivers some misty street
of very tall stern houses?
Giving me things the street is coming closer without smiling at me is it

O look, Susan, Peter and Glenn are here by the river
They are such fine overarm swimmers, I do not mind them,
I give them some of my things
Some hands take some things...

MY VIRTUOUS FRIEND

My virtuous friend comes in with her officer.
"We're going to where all is wonder and confusion,"
she cries, "to the top of the mountain!"
Her escort shrugs, his expression of drowsy fierceness
is not new to me. "So soon?" I say. He leans
against the wall, his uniform gold-braided at shoulder
and elbow, as one expects. "Why not?" he says.

"My spouse is a dreadfully unlucky man,"
says my friend, blowing kisses to her officer.
"Where is he?" I ask.
"Don't know, don't care!" How my virtuous friend
has changed!
"We're going to the top of the mountain!" she chants.
Her officer holds out both hands to me.
"No training is required," he says gently.
"All passions are virtues," he adds.

It lasts all winter, my friend, her officer
and me up on the mountain. Her officer cuts steps in the ice
so we can go in and out of the house by an upstair window,
for the lower storey is caught in a brace of snow.
We are very happy, until her cold-eyed husband
arrives with the thaw.

Poor Vanessa! Her thigh-booted husband
hefts my virtuous friend over his shoulder.

The river flows through the downstairs
like a very wise reflective floor. Upstairs
I turn to my officer. (But I will spare you
any more lurid details. I have to go
along this mortal path somehow. I can only tell you
so much.) Our officer? He has not found what he sought.

UNCLE NETTLETON

Uncle cooks me unusual dishes, strange soups.
Greedily we gobble the nasturtium broth.

"What a time to fall asleep,"
he sobs, "while painting my own portrait!"

"Can anything make you happy, Uncle?" I ask.
For answer he takes me walking by the hushed cold river
where Virginia Woolf drowned herself.

"No. It isn't haunted." He stares at the river,
chewing his sleeve defiantly.

"Can anything make you happy, Uncle?"
My uncle raises himself from the ground with a loving glance.

"Maybe," he says softly.

Under the little dark archway, he whispers,
"Will you be the harpist's bride, Kathy?"

"A possibility," he adds, "don't you think?"
But I am dreadfully afraid of his kisses.

"Furniture soon wears out,"
he fumes, hobbling indoors.

"Can anything make you happy, Uncle?"

He trembles in his green slippers,
rocking to and fro.

"Can anything make you happy?"

With a hunk of fivers in his hand,
he wheezes languishingly – "Kathy?"

In the privacy of his harp factory,
near the shavings bin, Uncle grips me hard.

"You are my true heir, beloved."

Uncle leans out of the bedroom window,
waving, blowing kisses. "O Kathy," he calls,
"at last I am happy..."

I run home, very sad, dodging the statues.
All night I watch trashy videos,
chainsmoking savagely and hoping I am not pregnant.

"O uncle dear," I sob, "will we get a good table
in the next world? What will they give us to eat there,
do you know?"

THE CYCLIST

She says goodbye to the river.
The two boys are driving the bullocks

out of the little field
and up the muddy lane.
She cycles to the baker's,

next door a long white curtain
bellies out of the pharmacy window,
she puts the long warm fragrant loaf

into her basket,
and rides on past
the charming gardens of French Street.

She sees a horse in a field
turn to a woman, a diva,
she wants everything

to keep on changing into something else,
dog change to owl, spider to ruby,
the sky darkening

like a scene from a minor judgement.
"Would he recognize me now?" she muses,
clenching the black-ribbed handlebars.

"It would give me great happiness
to destroy him with one thought,"
she pouts, pedalling faster.

"What good friends we would have been
if we were not man and wife!
O the mountains are high

and the moon is very small.
There was a bowl of violets
on the lid of the piano,

by the window he was kissing
my friend Anne Page.
When they saw me

they looked pained and sad.
Then he steered her towards the door
with a snarl of thwarted desire.

Poor boy, I said softly."

Now as she races over the bridge
the devil from heaven shouts down
to her,

yelling with unexpected tenderness,
"The truth is in they hands, Horatia!"

Fast and turbulent
falls the water over the tiny weir,
as she rides by.

Sandra Stevens

THE COMBINATION

It was his, her Xs, this overcoat,
heavy, outsize; he left it, she kept it,
kind of; after all, she'd bought him it,
at the infantschool jumble, 10p it cost,
she'd had to try it on a passing dad;
this coat, a heap on the floor, dumped;

And on it, dropped like it was nothing,
half a brick of Bath stone,
pale and soft and somehow snug,
nestling in the brown herring-bone
folds of the Harris-tweed coat.
These objects lie at ease together.

It acts on her like the deep
bare matter of suggestion:
stuff of life and death.

She knows a phoenix might rise
from such a nest. She feels only,
barely feels, the human truth
of the moving stillness of rubble.

Where's the man that filled the coat?
Where's the hand that held the brick?

The combination opens the heart.

Look, look, no blood, no blood.
Just this act of confrontation.

SIGNS OF WEAR

She sits on the doorstep
lips moving slightly
as with the other
end of a needle
she unpicks stitches
from a torn pullover

    Working says
    Done it all wrong
    Not worth a song

No kisses account for
her senseless mouthings
as with the frettings
of thread through fingers
she talks it over
for words undo feeling

    Worried sighs
    Long to forget
    Numb the regret

The sun shines through elder
the leaves untangle
as with a gesture
that's only natural
she lets drop freely
hands face tears love for life

    Wondering sees
    Bushed birds sing
    Take to the wing

JAMMAKER

She loved our damson tree.
The mass of white blossom.
The dark fruits veiled in bloom.
And she was such a jam maker...

She made pounds and pounds
and pounds of damson jam,
stirring and steaming
that rich heady smell
as strong and inexplicable
as the heart of a crimson rose
filling the kitchen, filling us
as she stirred and watched
and scooped the stones out
as they floated free of flesh
endlessly to the bubbling surface
and the jam darkened and thickened.
Then the saucer spoonful on the ledge
by the window to cool, blown across to see
if ripples formed, the stuff would set.
The warmed jars, the art of pouring
big full pans of scalding jam
clean into the pound jars,
then on with the waxed paper
and the cellophane tops, wet
on one side and rubber banded.
Last the labels, in her own hand.

Her exhaustion. The satisfaction.
The testing to taste if it was good.
And if it set hard
and needed cutting with a knife
and came out in firm chunks
sliced like jewels
she'd laugh and call it
damson cheese, a delicacy.

The jam of childhood.
What there always was

to put on our bread.
Granted not special then.

But such constant spells of love
stay sweet and last in the blood.

ZO: A REFLECTION

Even in the midst of parties (she's good at them
– like Woolf's Clarissa), the tang of salmon,
the bubble of champagne, she moves alone.

Those tender looks, the anxious intelligence,
are deeply familiar, from this woman
wrapped in strange scents of herbal medicine,

who offers the bone-to-bone gift of a hug,
and can still an ache with healing hands.

She performs a delicate poem
taking all the time it takes
giving it as she always does
the total focus of attention.

She leans giggling over the rayburn
caught in the repetition of old guilts.

Susan Taylor

PAULA

She paints
with her back against a wall
under the threat
of bailiffs hammering.

Her good tweed coat
is for sale
in a shop down the road
called 'Revival'.

She wraps, like fruits,
the generous cups and saucers,
hand thrown by a friend.
She knows a shop will deal in them.

She paints in primaries
directly from the paintbox,
draws at alarming speed
quick lines that flicker into truth.

No time to mix,
she works till 3 or 4 a.m.,
gets up at 8
for another day with her children.

I sit in front of a picture of hers
when I lose myself.
It is a garden
with a fountain full of flowers.

PINE

 Summer and Winter,
one Scot's Pine held this place,
put on the same umbrella
 of welcome.
I stood beneath its remembered shape,
a girl somehow out of Hardy,
waiting (fairly) coyly
 in the sunrise
for you to notice me
against a backdrop of cow parsley.
 Nothing happened,
we never stopped long enough
to be gentle beneath trees,
spoilt our chance with this one
now shafted by a storm.

NORTHERN LIGHTS

My father takes me out,
points over Bedlam Plantation
where the family's sheep
were so recently scrambling.

Here it is,
in swathes of milky violet,
a harvest of light
for our eyes wondering.

In Devon
I had kept watch impatiently,
night after night when they said
conditions were perfect.

I live too far South.
My father proves this
without words, by showing me
this flock in his Northern sky.

BE FALL

What lives behind the waterfall?
A snake that harbours earth and sky.

What lives beneath the waterfall?
Its single raindrop eye.

What lies before the waterfall?
A man of sticks and powers.

What lies below the waterfall?
A woman shaking creamy flowers.

What lies upon the waterfall?
A round of glass that cries out strong.

What lives about the waterfall?
The healing potency of song.

What lives within the waterfall?
The rainbow's quivering tongue.

LET

Mesmeric,
this dream has escaped
into a pocket of my life.
It wakes me long before dawn.
I sit out the darkness
to hear its silk running riot;
no need for finery
with this rustle
so near.

Here, sea is racing companion,
breaking like a great egg
into the ria's mouth
the surge
of its charge upstream
with wind all the way
through wizard locks
beating and whispering,
energy, energy.

Jane Tresidder

STORM

Sound
Cries
Inside the wind
Cloud is
A blunting
Hood
Of felt
Cowling
Over forms
Torn
For the last yard
Of a rainbow's arc,

Erratic march
Is a knife-dancer,
A sea-tease
Whose toes
Kick white.

Barren ships
Go for Newlyn
Drowning
Their bows.

The Lizard
Is a land
Of swallowed
Meadows
Or dissolving rocks
Before our eyes.

A hazardous peninsula
In sotto vocé
Supressed

Under
A warning horn.

IRISH TIM

Let me
Dream
In spring
Of one more
Careless entry
Into life.

To loose
The speed
Of daily time
And doze
For some
Unmeasured evening
Almost with you
In the hold
Of sleep.

Enclosed
By low
And mellowed walls
Silent
And sunk
In meadowed hills
Before
The fully
Fallen night.

Touch
My open hand
As tender light
Is moving
In your skin:-

And Irish Tim,
Just speak
A long
And lush
As river running slowly,

Never ending
Irish poem to me

FOR ANOTHER POET

The lines
Of our
Unwritten songs
Still gleam
At the rim
Of one
Unfilling cup.

All
My denials
Were taken away
As easily
As flowers
Out of
The unfenced meadows
Of this threat.

When
We are wise enough
To scatter them
Along the verges
Of the ways,
We learn
To be
The keepers
Of our own
Surrendered hearts.

April
Is all yours
For there is
A green season
Of being
So joyfully walking
In your man's
Light step.

AT THE FULMER PLACE

Friend
Of my freedom
Your wings
Are flying
In my arms,

Must
The scorch
Inside
Your
Cold, white feathers
Be a heart?

A knowing eye
As tender
As a fulmer's
Seems to float
In mine.

Oh, love,
I am your body
And you cannot
Leave my bones.

Over
The grief
Of my woman's
Emptiness,
This opalescent
Crucifix
Is dieing

Like
The shadow
Of a seabird
On the waves.

Irena Uderska

A WING AND A PRAYER

June is married
To the antipodes.
Starched bridal white
In her nurse's uniform
She enunciates her visa vows.
The one-eyed groom
Is impaled on a railing,
Incarcerated in a morgue.
Deportation is counted out
Pill by pernicious pill.

THE LAST SUPPER

The gnostic words
Lilt Greek,
Crumbs of food
From a rich feast.
An empty seat,
Bereft of its guest,
Has filled the pews,
A double indemnity
Beats the Yoruba drum.
Other voices speak,
Memories of April snows
Blanket the past,
Imprint the future.

HALLOW'EN

The pumpkin burns,
Scarring its tissue
With an inner flame.
Scooped out seeds
Tumble to the floor,
A vacuum feast
From a horn of plenty.
Eye sockets
Seer the darkness,
The nose is triangular,
A trinity of hope,
And the mouth is open,
Smiling in the fire light
It begs a kiss.

SNOW QUEEN

Eternity is the word,
Unspoken but heard.
You pierce it together,
A splinter at a time.
The glass is cracked,
A fragment has lodged
In your eye.
Your vision is blurred,
The rose no longer beautiful.

THE MADNESS OF MAUREEN FLATMAN

The madness of Maureen Flatman
Hangs unspoken
On every lip.
The shards
Of broken bottles
Line up
Alongside the potato peelings,
Missiles in a war
That no one
Will acknowledge.
The home front
Is sand-bagged
With silence,
The sirens
Of vitriolic abuse
Are received
With diplomatic deafness.
Mustard gas
Blinds compliant eyes
To burgled bombings.
The footprinted door
Swings on its hinges,
A visiting card
Torn at the edges.
A clerk in blue
Records the facts
And closes the file.
The madness of Maureen Flatman
hangs unspoken
On every lip.

Ruth Valentine

ASYLUM

In another country perhaps are emerald pines
dipping long fingers in a calm sea
and skies wrapping us lightly in long garments,
grapes ripening under leaves like a benediction.

And we will run
across borders beneath the vigilant
stars, and fall exhausted on dry earth
beneath ancient almonds, forgetting

we have brought our household gods with us on our backs,
and even under this rule of the scent of thyme
they go on exacting their daily tribute, at knifepoint.

PATRON SAINT

If you're going back, do me a favour,
take some gifts for me:

for my little sister, a crystallised apricot,
a pen for my father

and for my mother a silver St Christopher,
the one who carried a child across a river
and delivered him safely back to his parents' cottage,

and turned to go home and found the riverbank
on the far side defended with wire and guns.

IN PEACETIME

This is not the beach they clean at dawn
of the flotsam bodies of discarded partisans
from the other movement, the wrong kind of freedom.

This is not the island whose mango groves
shiver under the indifferent vigilance
of a moon that has seen the exile of thin stars.

And the ferry is not bringing marines landing
nor guns for cocaine at night. You can leave your door
unlocked, no jeeps will arrive before the dawn.

Close your eyes, spread out your arms, embrace the water.
If you dive you can hardly hear the fighter planes
low over the thyme-burnt hills, the practice mission.

BLOOD FEUD

We are proud inheritors of an ancient law
of gifts and revenge, the stranger
arriving at night on a tired horse
can command us anything, fruit, spirit, the stars.

If he dies shot on our land we remember him
with rifles and knife   and are remembered
with sword and rifle, one

dark-eyed boy, trembling
from his first love, first wine, sought out
in the lemon groves and the rocks. We send him

fiercely, with tears, to pay tribute to the mountains.
And never a man without crows circling his heart,
never a woman hanging out the sheets, singing.

Chris Banks lives a relatively peaceful existence in Somerset, despite the victims and warriors inhabiting her poems, and her possible Viking roots. She teaches in a college of FE, and works as a counsellor. One of Taunton's Fire River Poets, her work has appeared in magazines and the recent *Jewels & Binoculars* and *Iron Erotica* anthologies. Her first collection *Watching The Home Movies* was published by Odyssey in 1992.

Judi Benson is an American, resident in the U.K. since 1978. Obsessed with colour, she thinks she should have been a flower, though hopes to be a cat or horse when she grows up, but currently works part-time for the N.S.P.C.C. in a Child Protection unit. Her publications include *Somewhere Else* (Turret Books) and *In The Pockets Of Strangers* (Rockingham), and she co-edited Bloodaxe's *Klaonica: poems for Bosnia* with Ken Smith. She edits *Foolscap* magazine.

Stephanie Bowgett was born in Slough in 1950, brought up in Germany, and now teaches 10 & 11 year olds in Huddersfield. She started writing in 1991, and last year won prizes in the Arvon and Peterloo competitions. Together with three friends she organises monthly readings in 'The Albert', a town centre pub, and an anthology is planned for the near future. Slow Dancer are publishing a pamphlet of her work later in 1995.

Debjani Chatterjee was born in India and has also lived in Japan, Bangladesh, Hong Kong, Egypt and Morocco, before settling in England, where she is Director of the Oxfordshire Racial Equality Council. Her poetry books are *I Was That Woman* (Hippopotamus Press) and *The Sun Rises In The North* (Smith Doorstop), the latter jointly written with three other Northern writers. She has co-edited two bilingual anthologies for Bengali Women's Support Group, and also writes for children.

Alison Chisholm was born in Liverpool and now lives in Southport where she teaches speech and drama and creative writing, and is poetry tutor to the Southport Arts Centre. Widely published and anthologised, she has had five collections of poetry published, including *Paper Birds* (Stride, 1990), and is the author of *A Practical Poetry Course* and *The Craft Of Writing Poetry* (both Allison and Busby). She also contributes regularly to the poetry column in *Writers News*, and wrote the poetry course for The Writers College, Manchester. She is married with two daughters.

Rose Flint trained as a sculptor in London, then spent many years on the Welsh Borders before moving to Bath, where she now lives. She teaches Creative Writing, concentrating on Celtic mythology and environmental awareness, has twice been Poet in Residence for the Maelor Poetry Project, and is a tutor for the Taliesin Trust. Her collection *Blue Horse Of Morning* is published by Seren, and she is currently finishing a fantasy novel for children.

Jennie Fontana's first collection *Lost Stations* – written through ten years, three babies, and a marital breakdown – will be published by Stride in 1995. She believes that writing poetry and fiction help her towards 'a realization and grasping of self'. South East Arts awarded a major bursary for work on her first novel in 1993. Her freelance work involves 'putting the poetry back into people's lives'.

Linda France's work has appeared in two Bloodaxe collections – *Redi* and *The Gentleness Of The Very Tall*. She also edited their anthology *Sixty Women Poets*. She was born in Newcastle in 1958 and, after spending time in Dorset, Leeds, London and Amsterdam, she returned to the North East where she now works and lives with her two children. In 1993/4 she was awarded the first Arts Foundation Poetry Fellowship.

Sarah Hopkins was Poetry Editor of *Spare Rib* from 1982-5, and then also fiction editor for one year, while also Consulatant editor for *Tears In The Fence*. From 1978-9 she worked in *Wordcircus*, a performance group for women writers. Her poems have been widely published, as well as aired at public readings and performances. *Good Grief*, her first collection, was published by KQBX in 1992.

Libby Houston set out as a poet in 1961, when the influence of the American Beat movement had permeated Britain. Times change: she has now worked for several years as an Arvon tutor, at the same time also writing poems for children/BBC Schools Radio (published as the collection *All Change* [OUP, 1993]). "Honesty" is the concept that intrigues her as a poet, although she is also an ardent believer in poetry's musical/aural qualities. She currently lives in Bristol, and sometimes works as a botanist and typist. *Necessity* was published by Slow Dancer in 1988. "Next one always takes a long time."

Louise Hudson was born in 1958, lives in Devon with her two sons and runs *Fatchance* magazine. Her work has appeared in books, shop windows, on beer mats, tv and radio. She likes chocolate and lager (not neccessarily in that order). Her most recent book, *Intimate Relations*, was published by Stride.

Judith Kazantzis' most recent poetry collection is *The Rabbit Magician Plate* (Sinclair-Stevenson). *Making Advances, Selected Poems 1977-1992,* and a further collection, from which these poems are taken, will be published in 1995.

Mary Maher was born in Yorkshire and now lives in Devon. After spending many years in Special Education, where she concentrated on language development and communication difficulties, she started to write poetry. At this time she also became a subpostmistress and cidermaker. This year she is exploring North Devon's 'Tarka Trail' on foot and bike. Her books include *Dusting Round The Jelly* (Odyssey) and *Cold Flushes* (Stride).

Val Pancucci lives in South East London, and works part-time at the Centre of Medical Law and Ethics, King's College London. Her poems have appeared in various magazines, and in the anthologies *Floating Capital* (Potes & Poets Press) and *The Stumbling Dance* (Stride). Although eclectic in theme, her poems frequently explore psychological landscapes.

Mary Plain recently left Devon to do voluntary work in West Africa. She is a landscape painter, and an occasional poet, having had two pamphlets published. She has also written about art for magazines such as *Third Way* and *Event*, and was instrumental in setting up The Radical Women Artists' Fellowship.

Joan Poulson lives in Manchester where she is learning to play the flute, and enjoys as many concerts as possible – especially for cello. Recently she spent two years as Ariter In Residence in a psychiatric hospital. She writes poetry and drama, and is proud of having been the only non-Scouse scriptwriter for BBC radio soap *The Merseysiders*. Her work for children has appeared in almost forty anthologies worldwide; her collections are *Celebration* (UNICEF, 1993) and *Girls Are Like Diamonds* (OUP, 1994).

Wendy Richmond lives in Sheffield, where she runs writers workshops, lectures in screenwriting, and occasionally works as a storyteller. Her short film *Best Friends Ever* is currently doing the rounds of the festivals. Her four children are an endless resource for her writing, which has been widely published. For several years she edited the magazine *The Cutting Edge*.

Susan Sheppard grew up in Doddridge County, West Virginia. She has worked as a painter, a commercial artist, a horoscope columnist, and a teacher. She is the author of *Phoenix Cards*, a new-age card game; poems which have appeared in many literary journals and won awards; astrology articles which regularly appear in *Dell Horoscope*; and *The Colors We Shed*, a poetry collection in search of a publisher.

Penelope Shuttle lives in Cornwall with her husband Peter Redgrove and daughter Zoe. Her sixth collection of poetry, *Worse Things Than Divorce*, is in preparation. Her thematic interests are wide-ranging, and explore the sensuous and paradoxical realities of life. She believes in the imagination as a resource capable of redeeming, even now, our burdened and desecrate world, and regards poetry as a unique method of induction into the possibilities for transformation that still exist for us.

Sandra Stevens is a quester who'd rather be a streetwise existentialist or a cow in a field. She is drawn by silence, obsessed by language arts, and interested in people, nature, sun, rituals, pop culture, travel, religion, politics, the visual arts, gardens, walks, family, education, tv, and performance. She has performed live on tv, and radion and also works with women musicians as 'Silly Muse'. She co-ordinated Avon Poetry Festival for seven years, and her publications include *Words Between Spaces*, *The Weather Station*, and *Natural Break*.

Susan Taylor farmed in Lincolnshire for 15 years before moving to Devon to run the Arvon Foundation Centre at Totleigh Barton between 1981 and 1985. She is a founder member of Company of Poets and now lives on the Southern edge of Dartmoor with fellow poet Simon Williams and their two sons. Her most recent pamphlets are *A Binturong Bestiary* and *All In The Space Between*, a celebration of the work of sculptor Bridget McCrum.

Jane Tresidder grew up in Cornwall, studied painting at the Slade, and married Sam Carter – one of the tutors there. After becoming interested in Jung and sufism, and travelling to Cyprus to meet her sufi teacher, she returned to Cornwall: painting, writing, and studying singing in Mousehole. Her book *In The Mirror Of Your Eyes* was published by Stride.

Irena Uderska is a New Age party animal with a passion for history.

Ruth Valentine will soon be 50. She lives and works in North London. The poems included here come, somewhat obliquely, from her longstanding involvement with people in exile in the UK. Ruth's collection, *The Identification Of Species*, is available from Slow Dancer.

Acknowledgements:
Smith's Knoll, Spectrum, Fire River One,
Odyssey Press (Chris Banks);
Great River Review (Judi Benson);
Scratch, The Rialto, The Wide Skirt (Stephanie Bowgett)
PLN, Wasafari (Debjani Chatterjee);
Chester Poets Anthology, BBC Radio
Network Northwest (Alison Chisholm)
Tabla, New Welsh Review (Rose Flint);
Fatchance (Jennie Fontana);
Disability Arts Magazine,
Writing For Our Lives (Sarah Hopkins);
Slow Dancer, Circle Press (Libby Houston);
Slow Dancer, Odyssey, Iron (Louise Hudson);
Stand, Ambit (Judith Kazantzis);
Odyssey, Westwords (Mary Maher);
Scratch, Dog (Wendy Richmond);
Pennsylvania Review, Zone 3 (Susan Sheppard);
Passion (Penelope Shuttle).
Debjani Chatterjee's 'Visiting E.M. Forster'
won 2nd Prize in the 1992 Southport
Writers Circle Poetry Competition,
and her 'Words Between Us' was
Highly Commended in the Bournemouth
International Festival Poetry Competition 1992.
Rose Flint's 'Hill Of The Witch'
was 4th in the University of Wales'
Aberystwyth Competition.